United States Government Accountability Office

Report to Congressional Committees

August 2013

ARMY AND MARINE CORPS TRAINING

Better Performance and Cost Data Needed to More Fully Assess Simulation-Based Efforts

GAO-13-698

GAO Highlights

Highlights of GAO-13-698, a report to congressional committees

ARMY AND MARINE CORPS TRAINING

Better Performance and Cost Data Needed to More Fully Assess Simulation-Based Efforts

Why GAO Did This Study

The Army and Marine Corps use live and simulation-based training to meet training goals and objectives. Service officials have noted benefits from the use of simulation-based training—both in terms of training effectiveness and in cost savings or cost avoidance. A House report accompanying the bill for the National Defense Authorization Act for 2012 mandated GAO to review the status of the military services' training programs. This report follows GAO's reports on the Navy and Air Force, and assesses (1) changes in the Army's and Marine Corps' use of simulation-based training, including efforts to integrate live and simulation-based training capabilities; and (2) the factors the Army and Marine Corps consider in determining whether to use live or simulation-based training, including the extent to which they consider performance and cost information. GAO focused on a broad cross-section of occupations (e.g., aviation, armor, artillery), and analyzed service training strategies and other documents; and conducted six site visits and interviewed service officials involved with training and training development for the selected occupations.

What GAO Recommends

GAO recommends that the services develop metrics, and a methodology to compare live and simulation-based training costs. DOD partially concurred, but noted that it captures all relevant costs needed for decision making. GAO continues to believe the services may not be considering some important simulation-based training costs and a specific methodology is needed to more fully identify the universe of costs needed for comparison purposes.

View GAO-13-698. For more information, contact Sharon Pickup at (202) 512-9619 or pickups@gao.gov.

What GAO Found

Over the past several decades, the Army and Marine Corps have increased their use of simulation-based training—simulators and computer-based simulations. Historically, the aviation communities in both services have used simulators to train servicemembers in tasks such as takeoffs, and emergency procedures that could not be taught safely live. In contrast, the services' ground communities used limited simulations prior to 2000. However, advances in technology, and emerging conditions in Iraq and Afghanistan have led to increased use of simulation-based training in the ground forces. For example, in response to increases in vehicle rollovers, both services began using simulators to train servicemembers to safely evacuate vehicles. The services are also collaborating in the development of some simulation-based training devices. For instance, according to Marine Corps officials, the service reused 87 percent of the Army's Homestation Instrumentation Training System's components in its own training system, achieving about $11 million in cost avoidance and saving an estimated 7 years in fielding time. The services are also taking steps to better integrate live and simulation-based training, developing technical capabilities to connect previously incompatible simulation-based training devices. The Army's capability is now being fielded, and the Marine Corps' is in the initial development phase.

The Army and Marine Corps consider various factors in determining whether to use live or simulation-based training, but lack key performance and cost information that would enhance their ability to determine the optimal mix of training and prioritize related investments. As the services identify which requirements can be met with either live or simulation-based training or both, they consider factors such as safety and training mission. Also, they have cited numerous benefits of simulation-based training, such as improving servicemember performance in live training events, and reducing operating costs. Both services rely on subject matter experts, who develop their training programs, and after action reports from deployments and training exercises for information on how servicemembers may have benefited from simulation-based training. However, neither service has established outcome metrics to assist them in more precisely measuring the impact of using simulation-based devices to improve performance or proficiency. Leading management practices recognize that performance metrics can help agencies determine the contributions that training makes to improve results. Army and Marine Corps officials also generally consider simulation-based training to be less costly than live training and analyze some data, such as life cycle costs, when considering options to acquire a particular simulation-based training device. However, once simulation-based training devices are fielded, the services neither reevaluate cost information as they determine the mix of training nor have a methodology for determining the costs associated with simulation-based training. Federal internal control standards state that decision makers need visibility over a program's financial data to determine whether the program is meeting the agencies' goals and effectively using resources. Without better performance and cost data, the services lack the information they need to make more fully informed decisions in the future regarding the optimal mix of training and how best to target investments for simulation-based training capabilities.

_____ United States Government Accountability Office

Contents

Abbreviations

CATS	Combined Arms Training Strategies
DOD	Department of Defense
HMMWV	High-Mobility Multipurpose Wheeled Vehicle
LVC-IA	Live, Virtual, Constructive Integrating Architecture
MRAP	Mine Resistant Ambush Protected
PPBE	Planning, Programming, Budgeting, and Execution

GAO
U.S. GOVERNMENT ACCOUNTABILITY OFFICE

441 G St. N.W.
Washington, DC 20548

August 22, 2013

The Honorable Carl Levin
Chairman
The Honorable James M. Inhofe
Ranking Member
Committee on Armed Services
United States Senate

The Honorable Howard P. "Buck" McKeon
Chairman
The Honorable Adam Smith
Ranking Member
Committee on Armed Services
House of Representatives

For more than a decade, the Army and Marine Corps have focused their training on counterinsurgency and stability operations in order to meet challenges abroad. With the drawdown from Iraq now complete and the U.S. decreasing its military presence in Afghanistan, more forces are available for training and the services are transitioning to focus their training to once again emphasize a broader range of missions. At the same time, both services face constraints that can affect live training, such as limitations in maneuver space and access to ranges. As a result, they must find ways to maximize efficiency and cost-effectiveness in the use of their training resources. Both services have concluded that simulation-based training[1] can contribute to these aims and serve as a complement to live training.

---

[1]Training in a live environment involves real people operating real systems, e.g., an aviator flying an actual helicopter. Simulation-based training takes several forms. For example, virtual training involves real people operating simulated systems—specific devices that mimic actual equipment, such as a vehicle simulator. In constructive training, real people are trained using simulations—computer representations or imitations of reality. For example, the scene on a computer screen may look like contours on a map and the units and people are represented by icons. The services also use low cost gaming simulations. For the purposes of this report, simulation-based training will refer to all training that uses simulators or simulations, encompassing all virtual, constructive, and gaming training.

A report of the Committee on Armed Services, House of Representatives, which accompanied a bill for the National Defense Authorization Act for 2012, mandated that we review the status of the military services' training programs and report the results to the House and Senate Armed Services Committees.[2] For this review we assessed (1) changes in the Army's and Marine Corps' use of simulation-based training devices, including efforts to integrate live and simulation-based training capabilities; and (2) the factors the Army and Marine Corps consider in determining whether to use live or simulation-based training, including the extent to which they consider performance and cost information.

This is the third report we have produced to assess the services' mix of live and simulation-based training. In June 2012, we reported that the Navy had increased its emphasis on simulation-based training over the last decade, and had developed an overarching strategy that provided 12 investment priorities for simulation-based training.[3] In July 2012, we reported that the Air Force's approach to managing its virtual training efforts lacked (1) a designated organization with accountability and authority for achieving results and (2) an overarching strategy —key elements of an organizational framework —and, (3) a methodology for determining the costs of virtual training.[4] Accordingly, we recommended that the Air Force designate an entity to integrate its virtual training efforts, develop a strategy to align virtual training initiatives and goals, and develop a methodology to collect virtual training cost data. DOD concurred with our recommendations and identified actions that the Air Force planned to take.

To address our objectives, we met with officials involved in training and training development across both services and visited simulation-based training facilities. We focused our review to capture a significant portion of both services' training, by reviewing institutional and home station training and a broad cross-section of occupations that use simulation-based training devices. For both services, we selected the aviation, armor, and

---

[2]H.R. Rep. No. 112-78, at 111 (2011), which accompanied H.R. 1540, a bill for the National Defense Authorization Act for Fiscal Year 2012, Pub. L. No. 112-81 (2011).

[3]GAO, *Navy Training: Observations on the Navy's Use of Live and Simulated Training,* GAO-12-725R (Washington, D.C.: June 29, 2012).

[4]GAO, *Air Force Training: Actions Needed to Better Manage and Determine Costs of Virtual Training Efforts,* GAO-12-727 (Washington, D.C.: July 19, 2012).

artillery occupations. For the Army we also included infantry, and for the Marine Corps we also included amphibious assault vehicles and motor transport occupations.

To determine how the Army's and Marine Corps' use of simulation-based training devices has changed, including efforts to integrate live and simulation-based training capabilities, we analyzed service documents that provided information on the historical use of simulation-based training devices. We also interviewed officials representing the selected occupations and, among others, the services' training commands and materiel development organizations to discuss how simulators and simulations were and are currently being used. We evaluated guidance and documentation on the services' processes for coordinating their development of simulation-based training capabilities and technologies. In addition, we reviewed documents on the development of technical capabilities to connect simulation-based training devices. We also interviewed, and reviewed documents from, officials at Fort Hood, Texas—the first installation to field and use the Army's new technical capability for connecting live and simulation-based training—to discuss user assessments.

To ascertain the factors the Army and Marine Corps consider in determining whether to use live or simulation-based training, including the extent to which they consider performance and cost information, we reviewed DOD and service policies and guidance related to developing and conducting training. We also reviewed documentation on simulator usage data and met with officials from the services' training commands to discuss how this data was being used, and how the services determine the relationship between simulator usage and performance. In addition, we met with officials from Department of the Army and both services' training commands to determine how costs are considered and compared when developing the different mixes of live and simulation-based training. We reviewed training documents to determine how the services identified the mix of training for institutional and home station training. In addition, we reviewed leading management practices, the federal internal control standards, and our past reviews on the Navy's and Air Force's use of live and virtual training, and federal cost-estimating and budgeting guidance.

We conducted this performance audit from June 2012 to August 2013, in accordance with generally accepted government auditing standards. Those standards require that we plan and perform the audit to obtain sufficient, appropriate evidence to provide a reasonable basis for our findings and conclusions based on our audit objectives. We believe that the evidence obtained provides a reasonable basis for our findings and conclusions based on our audit objectives. For additional information on our scope and methodology, see appendix I.

Background

All Army and Marine Corps training —whether for individuals or units —is task-based, and each task has an associated set of conditions and standards. For example, the conditions may specify daytime or nighttime training, and the standard, a measure of a unit's or individual's proficiency in performing a task, could be to fire a weapon to become familiar with how it operates, or to put a specific number of rounds on target.

Active and reserve component servicemembers receive both institutional and home station training during the course of their career. Institutional training, which includes initial military training, subsequent professional military education, and leadership training, takes place at schoolhouses, i.e., Army centers of excellence and Marine Corps formal learning centers (which include recruit depots). Schoolhouses have designated training specialties, such as infantry, aviation, and artillery. For some occupations, the Army and Marine Corps train together at the same location. For example, both services train their armor and artillery occupations at Fort Benning, GA and Fort Sill, OK, respectively. During this training, instructors must closely follow a prescribed program of instruction so servicemembers can develop, refine, and improve individual skills to prescribed standards. The goal of institutional training is to ensure a common base of training and capability that can serve as a foundation for unit training.

Training at home station builds on the individual skills developed during institutional training. It begins with individual and small unit training and builds to large scale culminating training events that are designed to certify units for deployment.[5] Along the way, training complexity is increased incrementally by increasing the: task conditions (e.g., adding nighttime training); training tempo; number of tasks; or, number of personnel.

---

[5]A culminating training event is a large scale training exercise that occurs prior to deployment or after a series of smaller training events. The event is individually tailored to support and assess a unit's ability to perform tasks.

Like type units, e.g., all infantry platoons, all Apache helicopter squadrons, or all Stryker brigade combat teams, train on many of the same tasks. However, unit commanders are ultimately responsible for their units' training, and a variety of factors can lead commanders to adopt different approaches to training. For example, when units are scheduled to deploy, commanders may adjust their training based on their units' assigned missions or deployment locations.

Army and Marine Corps Have Increased the Use of Simulation-Based Training and Taken Steps to Collaborate on Development Efforts

Over the last several decades, the Army and Marine Corps have incorporated simulators and simulations more broadly into training and are collaborating in the development of these devices. The two services are also taking steps intended to increase the interoperability of simulators and simulations and support training across live and simulation-based training environments.

The Services' Use of Simulation-Based Training Devices Has Increased and They Are Collaborating in Device Development

The Army's and Marine Corps' use of simulation-based training devices has increased over time, and the services have collaborated in developing some devices. Simulation-based training devices were first incorporated into training for aircraft and later incorporated into the ground communities. Both services' aviation communities have used simulators for more than half a century. In addition to training tasks that could not be trained in an actual aircraft, such as emergency procedures, the services currently use flight simulators to train new pilots on tasks such as take-offs and landings, and to provide refresher training to more experienced pilots.

The services' ground communities did not begin using simulators and simulations until later. Specifically, until the 1980s, training in the ground communities was primarily live training. Then, to enhance live, force on force training, the Army began using a laser training device that simulated weapons fire. In addition, both services began using simulations for the purpose of training higher-level commanders and their staffs in command and control and decision making.

Further advances in technology resulted in the acquisition of simulators and simulations with additional capabilities designed to help servicemembers and units acquire and refine skills through more concentrated and repetitive training. For example, during the 1990s, the Army introduced more advanced trainers for its ground and aviation forces. In addition, the Marine Corps began using devices that allowed individual marines to conduct training in basic and advanced marksmanship, shoot/no-shoot judgment, and weapons employment tactics. More recently, during operations in Iraq and Afghanistan, both services introduced a number of new simulators and simulations to prepare servicemembers for conditions on the ground and emerging threats. For example, to provide initial and sustainment driver training, the Army and Marine Corps began using simulators that can be reconfigured to replicate a variety of vehicles. In addition, in response to an increase in vehicle rollovers, both services began using egress trainers to train servicemembers to safely evacuate their vehicles.

As the Army and Marine Corps have continued to expand their use of simulation-based training, they have collaborated on the development of some simulation-based training devices. For example, the Army uses the Homestation Instrumentation Training System to support collective maneuver training for platoon through battalion units. In developing a similar training system— the Marine Corps Instrumentation Training System —the service determined that it could reuse 87 percent of the components in the Army's system.[6] As a result, officials told us, the Marine Corps achieved approximately $11 million in cost avoidance and fielded the system in 2 years instead of the projected 9 years. In turn, the Marine Corps developed enhancements for its own training system that the Army has incorporated into its fielded version of the Homestation Instrumentation Training System. Further, the Army and Marine Corps determined that they had a similar need for terrain maps of Iraq and Afghanistan in their simulators. Rather than each service acquiring their own, the Army and Marine Corps share the same version of Virtual Battlespace 2, a gaming capability, resulting in shared development costs and content. In addition, the Army's and Marine Corps' training materiel developers, who are collocated in Orlando, Florida,[7] have established memorandums of understanding intended to promote coordination and

---

[6]The Army's Homestation Instrumentation Training System and the Marine Corps' Instrumentation Training System are capable of monitoring real-time live training and exercises for the purposes of data collection, analysis, and review. The systems provide data and analysis of unit performance in various training situations, such as force on force.

[7]The primary simulation and training acquisition and sustainment organizations for each of the four services are located in Orlando, Florida.

encourage maximum reusability of existing devices. Table 1 provides examples of simulators and simulations currently being used in the Army and Marine Corps aviation and ground communities.

Table 1: Examples of Army and Marine Corps Simulators and Simulations

Name	Purpose	Simulator or Simulation[a]	Service
Virtual Battlespace 2	To allow a unit to train together in a number of environments against a virtual opposing force.	Simulation	Army and Marine Corps
Close Combat Tactical Trainer	To provide armor, infantry, cavalry, and reconnaissance crews, units, and staffs with a collective training capability.	Simulator	Army
Aviation Combined Arms Tactical Trainer	To support unit collective and combined arms training for multiple helicopter platforms such as the Blackhawk and the Apache.	Simulator	Army
Indoor Simulated Marksmanship Trainer	To provide the capability to train in basic and advanced marksmanship; can be reconfigured to replicate multiple weapons.	Simulator	Marine Corps
Family of egress simulators (For example, High-mobility multipurpose wheeled vehicle (HMMWV) and mine resistant ambush protected (MRAP) vehicle egress simulator)	To develop the skills necessary to survive a vehicle rollover.	Simulator	Army and Marine Corps
Common Driver Trainer, Operator Driver Simulator	To teach servicemembers how to drive selected vehicles, such as the HMMWV and MRAP.	Simulators	Army and Marine Corps, respectively
Combined Arms Command and Control Trainer Upgrade System	Allows commanders and their staff to train or rehearse tactics, techniques, procedures and decision making processes in a realistic, scenario driven environment.	Simulation	Marine Corps

Source: GAO analysis of Army and Marine Corps information.

[a] A simulator is a specific device that mimics actual equipment, e.g. a vehicle simulator. A simulation is a computer representation or imitation of reality.

The Army and Marine Corps Are Taking Steps Intended to Better Integrate Live and Simulation-Based Training Capabilities

As the Army and Marine Corps continue integrating simulation-based devices into their training, they are taking steps intended to increase interoperability and support training across live and simulation-based training environments. The Army's live, virtual, and constructive capabilities were largely incompatible and operators at individual installations had to develop technical workarounds to connect these capabilities in a single realistic home station training exercise. According to Army officials, these workarounds are temporary and require significant time and manpower to prepare for each exercise, which limits the availability of simulator operators to support other training needs on an installation. In an effort to overcome the need for temporary solutions and more fully integrate live, virtual, and constructive training, the Army began developing the Live, Virtual, Constructive Integrating Architecture (LVC-IA) in 2005. The LVC-IA is a technical capability that provides common protocols, standards, and interfaces to standardize existing incompatible devices across installations and facilitate interoperability without workarounds. According to the Army, the integrated training environment—facilitated by the LVC-IA —will support unit live and simulation-based training at the brigade level and below; expand the training area and mitigate constraints imposed by limited maneuver space and environmental restrictions; and allow units to replicate the complexities of the operating environment. Since September 2012, the Army has fielded the LVC-IA capability at four installations and expects to field it to a total of 18 Army installations by the end of fiscal year 2017. Currently, the LVC-IA connects three simulators and simulations, although service officials told us that they plan to incorporate additional devices, including those of other services, when they field future versions of the LVC-IA.[8]

To facilitate the integration of live and simulation-based training devices in the Marine Corps, the service is currently in the conceptual phase of development for its Live, Virtual and Constructive Training Environment. The Marine Corps' intent is to eventually combine any of the three training environments (live, virtual and constructive) to create a common environment by which units can seamlessly interact as though they are physically located together. After assessing the Army's LVC-IA, the Marine Corps concluded that the capabilities identified by the Army were beneficial to the Marine Corps; however, it did not address all of the capabilities needed to meet the unique training requirements of the Marine Corps, such as the need to train across environments while embarked aboard naval vessels. According to Marine Corps officials, they are monitoring the Army's LVC-IA initiative to leverage applicable technology and lessons learned.

---

[8]The LVC-IA currently connects the Homestation Instrumentation Training System, the Close Combat Tactical Trainer, and the Aviation Combined Arms Tactical Trainer, and constructive simulations.

The Army and Marine Corps Consider Various Factors in Determining the Mix of Live and Simulation-Based Training, But Lack Key Information to Assess the Impact and Cost of Simulation-Based Training

The Army and Marine Corps consider various factors —such as safety, and training objective or mission—in determining whether to use live or simulation-based training to meet training requirements. However, the services do not have information on performance and cost that would assist them in assessing and comparing the benefits of simulation-based training as they seek to optimize the mix of training to meet requirements and prioritize related investments. For example, regarding home station training, they collect some information on usage of simulation-based training devices, and the Army's training materiel developer is conducting a study to determine the benefits of training specific tasks using simulations. However, neither service has developed overall metrics or indicators that can be used on a service-wide basis to measure how the use of simulation-based training devices contributes to improving the effectiveness of training. In addition, the services have not developed a methodology to identify the costs associated with using simulation-based training.

The Services Consider Various Factors to Determine When Live and Simulation-Based Training Can or Will Be Used

The Army and Marine Corps identify requirements and develop related programs of instruction for institutional training, and overarching training strategies for home station training. In developing the programs of instruction and overarching training strategies, officials identify which requirements can be met with live or simulation-based training and which can be met using a combination of both types of training. Each type of training has certain advantages. For example, live training allows servicemembers to become familiar with the feel and use of actual weapons or equipment, adjust to uncertain conditions that can change quickly, such as weather, and work together in teams in a more realistic environment. Simulation-based training allows servicemembers to quickly replicate a wide variety of conditions that may not exist on a live training range, such as terrain differences. It also allows individuals and units to conduct numerous iterations to master a task (an option that may not be viable in a live training environment); reduces required equipment maintenance; and provides instant feedback on performance.

To leverage the advantages associated with both types of training and determine whether to use live or simulation-based training, officials from the services consider a number of factors, such as: training objective or mission; safety of servicemembers conducting the training and the safety of the general public; required training frequency for the task; available training time; the need to replicate environmental conditions, e.g., weather conditions; availability of training ranges, simulators, and simulations; and realism of existing simulators and simulations, including their concurrency.[9] According to Army officials and Marine Corps training guidance, when deciding whether to use simulation-based training, the primary consideration is improving the quality of training and the state of readiness; potential cost savings or avoided costs are an important, but secondary, consideration.

In developing programs of instruction for institutional training, Army and Marine Corps subject matter experts, who in many cases have prior service experience, determine which training tasks will be conducted live, and which will be met using simulation-based training. For example, Army aviators learning to fly an Apache helicopter must train for about 55 hours in a simulation-based environment and about 84 hours in a live environment. In the same way the Marine Corps prescribes about 66 hours of live training and about 272 hours of simulation-based training for one of its artillery courses.

For home station training, the services provide unit commanders with various guidance documents to assist them in developing their unit training plans. However, the services do not prescribe the environment in which home station training should be conducted. Instead, both services allow unit commanders to decide whether to use live or simulation-based training or a mix of both types of training. While unit commanders have this discretion, available training time, and the availability of ranges, ammunition, and simulation-based training devices may influence their decisions concerning their units' mix of training.

The Army provides guidance to unit commanders through its Combined Arms Training Strategies (CATS) and the Marine Corps through Training and Readiness Manuals. The Army's CATS identify the tasks to be trained; purpose; outcomes; training audience; and event duration and frequency. The CATS also identify which requirements should be conducted through live training and which can be conducted using a combination of live and simulation-based training. They also identify the simulators or simulations that could be used. Similarly, the Marine Corps' Training and Readiness Manuals identify the critical tasks and associated standards to which the tasks should be trained; prerequisite training events; the internal and external support necessary to complete an event;

---

[9]Concurrency refers to the extent to which simulators match the most current aspects of the weapons systems they are designed to replicate.

as well as the simulation-based training devices that can be used. In some instances, the Marine Corps manuals are more specific than the Army CATS because they contain simulation codes that specify when a simulator or simulation must, should, or can be used, as well as when no simulation-based training device is available. However, there are very few instances where the manuals specify that simulation-based training must be used. Both services' training strategies recommend that servicemembers and units use simulators or simulations to build and maintain proficiency prior to qualifying for many tasks in a live training environment.

Like the Army and Marine Corps, the Air Force and Navy recognize that effective training requires a mix of live and simulation-based training and some live training events cannot or should not be replaced by a simulator. As we previously reported,[10] the Navy and Air Force have identified mixes of live and simulation-based training and in some cases are more prescriptive with regard to simulation-based training and their investments in these training technologies. In particular, the Air Force has identified the percentage of events that can be completed in a simulator and the Navy's Overarching Fleet Training Simulator Strategy contains specific guiding principles for simulator use. For example, one principle states that training simulators should be used to replace live training to the maximum extent possible where training effectiveness and operational readiness are not compromised. Another states that if a skill or talent can be developed or refined, or if proficiency can effectively and efficiently be maintained in a simulator, then a simulator should be used. Furthermore, recognizing the constrained fiscal environment and pressure on defense accounts, the strategy lists 12 investment priorities, including investing in simulators and simulations that have the greatest potential to generate cost savings, and it assigns responsibility for developing a methodology for tracking return on simulator investments.

---

[10]GAO-12-725R and GAO-12-727.

The Army and Marine Corps Cite Benefits of Simulation-Based Training, but Lack Information to Evaluate Impacts on Performance and Cost

Army and Marine Corps training documents and officials from both services have noted benefits from the use of simulation-based training — both in terms of training effectiveness and in terms of cost savings or cost avoidance. According to various documents from both services, training in a simulation-based environment complements necessary live training and allows the fundamentals to be practiced in a more cost-effective manner. Further, simulation-based training allows servicemembers to quickly replicate a wide variety of conditions, receive instant feedback on performance, and conduct multiple iterations to master a task. In addition, training with simulation-based devices can improve training efficiency by: controlling costs by expanding the number of training sites; reducing training time; improving safety and reducing equipment wear and tear; reducing or offsetting training ammunition requirements and/or operating tempo costs; and reducing the need for additional training land. Finally, training officials from both the Army and the Marine Corps noted the improved performance of servicemembers in a live training environment as a result of the increased use of simulation-based training. However, the services lack information to assist them in better determining how the use of simulation-based training devices contribute to improved performance and evaluating the costs of simulation-based training.

Army and Marine Corps Collect Some Data on Simulation-Based Training but Lack Metrics to Assess Impact on Performance

While the Army and Marine Corps currently collect data on the usage of simulators and the Army is conducting a study to gain insight into how simulation-based training contributes to training, neither service has established metrics or indicators to assist them in more broadly measuring the impact of simulation-based training on improving the performance or proficiency of servicemembers. As the services look at ways to optimize the use of training resources, such information could be useful to guide decisions on the optimal mix of live and simulation-based training during the training development process, and as commanders exercise discretion in how best to integrate the use of simulators during home station training. Specifically, we found that the services collect utilization data to manage the scheduling and distribution of simulation-based training devices across installations to support home station training. For example, on a monthly basis, both the Army and Marine Corps collect data on the number of hours simulators are used and throughput (i.e., the number of soldiers or marines who use a simulator), and in some cases, the number of virtual rounds fired or miles driven. Further, in the case of the Army, the services' training materiel developer is currently conducting a study to determine the benefits of simulation-based training. Specifically, the Program Executive Office for Simulations, Training, and Instrumentation, is compiling case studies to demonstrate the benefits and impacts of training certain tasks using simulations. The intent of this study is to evaluate how training with simulation-based devices compares to training without these devices. The Army's study, which it expects to release later in 2013, as well as the utilization data both services are collecting, could be useful in establishing metrics to help optimize the services' use of their training resources. Neither service has taken steps to identify performance metrics and the type of performance data that would be needed to evaluate how the use of simulation-based training devices contributes to training effectiveness. Officials told us they recognize the value of performance metrics, but given the pace of operations in Iraq and Afghanistan over the past several years, priority was focused on conducting training and preparing forces to deploy. Officials further noted that some training tasks are subjective, making it difficult to develop specific, quantifiable metrics, and that different devices may require different sets of metrics to reflect how their use contributes to improved performance. Currently, in the absence of performance data, the services obtain information on the contribution of simulation-based training from subject matter experts, who are responsible for developing training programs of instruction and overarching strategies, as well as information based on feedback and after action reports from deployments and training exercises.

As previously noted, the Navy has identified guiding principles for simulator use, including a principle that notes the need to quantifiably demonstrate how simulator use contributes to achieving training objectives. Further, leading management practices recognize, when designed effectively, performance measures help decision makers (1) determine the contributions that training makes to improve results, (2) identify gaps in performance, and (3) determine where to focus resources to improve results.[11] In particular, incorporating valid measures of effectiveness, i.e., outcome measures, into training programs would enable an organization to better ensure that desired changes will occur in trainees' skills, knowledge, and abilities. We recognize and have previously reported that it is difficult to establish performance measures

---

[11]GAO, *Human Capital: A Guide for Assessing Strategic Training and Development Efforts for the Federal Government*, GAO-04-546G (Washington, D.C.: March 2004).

for outcomes that are not readily observable.[12] However, without a means to determine how the use of simulation-based training devices contribute to improved performance, decision makers in the Army and Marine Corps lack information to make informed decisions about the optimal mix of training.

Army and Marine Corps Lack a Methodology for Identifying Costs Related to Simulation-Based Training

Army and Marine Corps officials stated they generally consider simulation-based training less costly than live training; however, neither service has established a methodology to identify and compare the costs associated with live and simulation-based training. According to federal internal control standards, decision makers need visibility over a program's financial data to determine whether the program is meeting the agencies' goals and effectively using resources.[13] On the basis of past reviews of federal cost-estimating and budgeting guidance,[14] we have determined that a key principle for evaluating cost estimates is ensuring that all significant costs are included.[15] In our previous report on the Air

---

[12]GAO, *State Partnership Program: Improved Oversight, Guidance, and Training Needed for National Guard's Efforts with Foreign Partners*, GAO-12-548 (Washington, D.C.: May 2012); GAO, *Results-Oriented Government: GPRA Has Established a Solid Foundation for Achieving Greater Results*, GAO-04-38 (Washington, D.C.: Mar. 10, 2004); and *Performance Measurement and Evaluation: Definitions and Relationships*, GAO-11-646SP (Washington, D.C.: May 2011).

[13]GAO, *Standards for Internal Control in the Federal Government*, GAO/AIMD-00-21.3.1 (Washington, D.C.: Nov. 1, 1999).

[14]GAO, *Military Bases: Opportunities Exist to Improve Future Base Realignment and Closure Rounds*, GAO-13-149 (Washington, D.C.: March 2013). GAO has previously reviewed numerous federal guidance documents related to cost estimating, accounting standards, economic analysis, and budgeting, and identified key principles that we believe can be applied to the evaluation of cost-savings estimates. Two of those four principles include having an appropriate level of detailed documentation such that a reasonably informed person could easily recreate, update, or understand the cost estimate, and all significant costs and key assumptions should be included in the cost estimate. The guidance documents we reviewed include: GAO, *GAO Cost Estimating and Assessment Guide: Best Practices for Developing and Managing Capital Program Costs*, GAO-09-3SP (March 2009); Office of Management and Budget Circular No. A-11, *Preparation, Submission and Execution of the Budget* (August 2011, superseded by an August 2012 issuance); Federal Accounting Standards Advisory Board, *Statement of Federal Financial Accounting Standards 4* (June 2011); Department of Defense Instruction 7041.3, *Economic Analysis for Decisionmaking* (Nov. 7, 1995); and Department of Defense Financial Management Regulation 7000.14-R, vol. 4, ch. 22, *Cost Finding* (May 2010). We believe that these documents collectively contain broad themes that can be applied to evaluating cost analyses.

[15]GAO-12-727.

Force's use of live and virtual training, for instance, we reported that the Air Force had estimated it could realize savings in its training program by reducing live flying hours and taking other steps, such as increasing the use of virtual training. However, the Air Force did not have a complete picture of costs related to virtual training. For example, it had excluded certain costs from its estimates, such as expenses for aircrew travel to simulator locations, additional contractor personnel to schedule and operate simulators, and the purchase of additional simulators to meet increased demand. Therefore, we recommended that the Air Force develop a methodology to determine the universe of costs and a means to collect and track data in order to enhance its ability to make future investment decisions about the mix of live and virtual training. DOD concurred with our recommendation and noted that the Air Force is developing a standard methodology of accounting and tracking cost categories associated with live and simulation-based training.

In general, the Army and Marine Corps collect and assess some costs associated with the use of simulation-based training devices as part of their acquisition and budgeting processes. For example, both services conduct cost benefit analyses—including a review of estimated simulator and simulation life-cycle costs, such as development costs and costs to dispose of a device at the end of its life—as they make acquisition decisions such as whether to develop new simulation-based training devices. In addition, after the simulator or simulation is acquired and fielded, the services consider the life-cycle cost to operate and maintain them as they identify the funding needs to be considered in the budget development process. However, they do not reevaluate cost information during their training development process as they determine which training should be conducted live and which can be conducted using a combination of live and simulation-based training. Further, at this point in time, neither service has a methodology for identifying the universe of costs associated with using simulation-based devices or a means to collect and track these costs.

According to Army and Marine Corps officials, additional cost information would be useful in making decisions on the mix of training and related investment decisions. During the course of our work, some officials cited examples of specific costs that could be considered and variables that might need to be taken into account in developing an approach to comparing simulation-based and live training. For example, some officials noted that ammunition costs could be considered significant to both types of training, but that there are some variables to be considered in comparing these costs. For instance, they noted that the number of virtual rounds fired in a simulator could be compared to the cost of live ammunition, but that there are limits to this type of comparison because units can fire more rounds in a simulator than they would be allocated during live training. As a result, a one-to-one comparison does not present a totally accurate picture of the potential costs that are saved or avoided when conducting simulation-based training rather than live training. Additionally, they noted that ammunition has a shelf life. If it is not used within its available shelf life the services can incur costs to demilitarize the ammunition. Therefore, firing live ammunition that is approaching the end of its shelf life may actually result in cost avoidance rather than an additional cost for the services. In addition, they noted that comparing the costs of fuel and spare parts of an aircraft used in live training to the cost of technicians and spare parts needed to maintain simulators would not provide an accurate comparison if the costs of facilities, utilities, and training personnel to support the simulators were not included as well. These costs and variables could serve as the foundation for developing a cost methodology. Without a means to assess the impact of using simulators on performance and to compare the costs associated with live training and the use of simulation-based training devices, decision makers in the Army and Marine Corps lack information to make fully informed decisions in the future regarding the optimal mix of training and related investment decisions.

Conclusions

As the Army and Marine Corps take steps to further integrate the use of simulation-based training with live training, and collaborate on development efforts in a fiscally constrained environment, both services are facing important decisions regarding how to adapt current approaches to meet training requirements and prioritize related investments, including those related to the acquisition of simulation-based training capabilities. While both services have noted benefits from the use of simulation-based training —in terms of training effectiveness and in cost savings or cost avoidance, it is important that they have valid performance and cost data to assist them in evaluating these benefits. We recognize that both services currently collect various types of information on the use of simulation devices and consider costs to a certain extent in their acquisition and budgeting processes. However, taking additional steps to expand these efforts by establishing performance-oriented metrics and a methodology to identify the costs associated with simulation-based training would provide them greater insights into how the use of simulation-based training contributes to improved performance or proficiency of servicemembers, and a point of comparison for assessing the cost implications of using simulation-based or live training. Moreover, until the Army and Marine Corps take actions to increase their visibility over the impact of simulation-based training on performance and costs, they will continue to lack key information that could assist them in determining how to optimize the mix of live and simulation-based training in the future and target simulation-based training investments on the devices that have the greatest potential to improve mission performance.

Recommendations for Executive Action

To improve decision makers' abilities to make fully informed decisions concerning whether training requirements can be met with live and simulation-based training and determine optimal mixes of live and simulation-based training, we recommend that the Secretary of Defense direct the Secretary of the Army and the Commandant of the Marine Corps to take the following two actions:

- Develop outcome-oriented performance metrics that can be used to assess the impact of simulation-based training on improving the performance or proficiency of servicemembers and units.
- Develop a methodology—to include identifying the costs that should be included and how these costs should be captured—for comparing the costs associated with the use of live and simulation-based training.

Agency Comments and Our Evaluation

In written comments on a draft of this report, DOD partially concurred with our recommendations. In response to our recommendation that the Secretary of Defense direct the Secretary of the Army and the Commandant of the Marine Corps to develop outcome-oriented performance metrics that can be used to assess the impact of simulation-based training on improving the performance or proficiency of servicemembers and units, DOD agreed that an enhancement in outcome-oriented performance metrics would be helpful in the decision-making process. DOD noted that given the magnitude and scope of training tasks, varying competencies of the training audience, and ever changing technology, the problem set contains many independent variables. DOD said that it will study the problem set, and as appropriate, develop a construct and implementation plan to include performance metrics to assess the impact of simulation-based training on improving the performance or proficiency of servicemembers and units. We recognize that DOD must consider many independent variables and note in our report that some training tasks are subjective, making it difficult to develop specific, quantifiable metrics. However, facing these same types of challenges, we describe in our report that the Navy has a simulator strategy that notes the need to quantifiably demonstrate how simulator use contributes to achieving objectives. Further, as noted in our report, Army and Marine Corps training tasks already have associated conditions and standards. These standards could be used as the basis for developing performance metrics to evaluate differences, if any, between live and simulation-based training effectiveness. As both services have noted anecdotal benefits from the use of simulation-based training, we continue to believe that establishing performance-oriented metrics would provide the Army and Marine Corps with greater insights into how the use of simulation-based training contributes to improved performance or proficiency.

DOD partially concurred with our recommendation that the Secretary of Defense direct the Secretary of the Army and the Commandant of the Marine Corps to develop a methodology—to include identifying the costs that should be included and how these costs should be captured—for comparing the costs associated with the use of live and simulation-based training. In its comments, DOD noted that the Army and Marine Corps capture all relevant costs needed for decision-making during the Planning, Programming, Budgeting, and Execution (PPBE) process in procuring simulators/simulation devices. DOD further stated that the Marine Corps training is based on the Systems Approach to Training, which includes policy on developing outcome-oriented performance metrics that are employed in school house lesson plans and home station training. DOD noted that the combination of PPBE and the Systems Approach to Training ensures that costs are considered in determining the mix of live and simulation-based training. DOD further stated that the Army and Marine Corps concur that a more comprehensive cost analysis would assist decision making in determining the optimal mix of live and simulation-based training. DOD did not cite any specific steps that the services plan to take. In our report, we specifically recognize that the Army and Marine Corps assess costs associated with simulation based devices, such as life cycle costs, as they make acquisition decisions and during their budget development process when they determine funding needs to operate acquired devices. However, the services do not reevaluate cost information during their training development process which is the point at which they are determining the mix of live and simulated based training. Furthermore, beyond those costs currently assessed in the budget process, we found examples of additional costs that could be considered if the services were to perform a cost comparison analysis between live and simulated based training, such as facilities, fuel and ammunition. Therefore, to enhance their ability to optimize the mix of training and better understand related cost implications, we continue to believe the services need to expand their current efforts and take specific steps to develop a methodology for comparing costs associated with the use of live and simulated based training. DOD's comments are included in their entirety in appendix II. DOD also provided technical and clarifying comments, which we have incorporated where appropriate.

We are sending copies of this report to appropriate congressional committees, the Secretary of Defense, the Secretary of the Army, and the Commandant of the Marine Corps. In addition, this report will be available at no charge on our website at http://www.gao.gov.

If you or your staff have any questions about this report, please contact me at (202) 512-9619 or pickups@gao.gov. Contact points for our Offices of Congressional Relations and Public Affairs may be found on the last page of this report. GAO staff who made major contributions to this report are listed in appendix III.

Sharon L. Pickup
Director
Defense Capabilities and Management

Appendix I: Scope and Methodology

To address our objectives, we met with officials from the Office of the Secretary of Defense, the Department of the Army Headquarters, Marine Corps Headquarters, and several Army and Marine Corps commands and organizations, and visited simulation-based training facilities. Our review focused on the mix of live and simulation-based training for institutional and home station training because this training represents a significant portion of both services' training. Excluded from this review were live and simulation-based training at the services' combat training centers and during deployment. We selected Army and Marine Corps occupations that use the largest number of simulation-based training devices and represent a broad cross-section of how these devices are used by the services, respectively. For both the Army and Marine Corps, we selected the aviation, armor, and artillery occupations. In addition, for the Army we included infantry, and for the Marine Corps we included amphibious assault vehicles and motor transport occupations. We held discussions with training officials representing each of these occupations. In addition, we visited the Army Aviation Center of Excellence in Fort Rucker, Alabama; the Army Maneuver Center of Excellence at Fort Benning, GA, where both services train their armor personnel; and Fort Sill, Oklahoma, where both services train their artillery personnel.

To determine how the Army's and Marine Corps' use of simulation-based training devices has changed since the services first began using simulators, we reviewed and analyzed service briefings and documentation that provided information on the historical use of simulation-based training devices, and the timelines within which simulators for various occupations became available. In addition, we interviewed officials from the Department of the Army-Management Office for Training Simulations; Marine Corps Plans, Policies and Operations; and the services' training commands —the Army's Training and Doctrine Command and the Marine Corps' Training and Education Command—to discuss how simulators and simulations were and are currently being used. We also interviewed officials representing the selected service occupations and from the Army Reserve Command, the Army National Guard, and Marine Corps Forces Reserve, to discuss the mix of live and simulation-based training, how the use of simulators and simulations has evolved, and the benefits, limitations, and challenges of simulation-based training. Additionally, we reviewed our prior reports to gain additional perspective on how simulators and simulations were used in the past. To assess the Army's and Marine Corps' efforts to better integrate live and simulation-based training, we evaluated documentation on simulation-based training technologies and capabilities. In addition, we met with officials from the Army's and Marine Corps' training commands and materiel development organizations—the Program Executive Office for Simulations, Training, and Instrumentation and the Program Manager for Training Systems, respectively—to discuss how they coordinate the development of simulation-based training capabilities and technologies and ongoing initiatives to further integrate simulation-based training. We also obtained and reviewed guidance and documentation from both services related to the development of certain technical capabilities to connect incompatible simulation-based training devices—the Army's Live, Virtual, and Constructive—Integrated Architecture (LVC-IA), and the Marine Corps' Live, Virtual and Constructive Training Environment. We discussed these technical capabilities with officials from the Army headquarters, and the services' training commands and materiel development organizations. In addition, we reviewed Army documents on the LVC-IA and the summary of the findings and lessons learned from the initial fielding of the integrated architecture at Fort Hood, Texas. We also interviewed officials from Fort Hood, including company, battalion, and brigade-level officials from the 2nd Brigade Combat Team, 1st Cavalry Division, to discuss their perspectives on the benefits and challenges related to the initial LVC-IA exercise. Additionally, we reviewed Marine Corps' documents, such as its Live, Virtual and Constructive Training Environment Initial Capabilities Document; and the Training and Education Modeling and Simulation Master Plan 2010. We also interviewed Marine Corps training officials to obtain information on the purpose and current state of its Live, Virtual and Constructive Training Environment.

To ascertain the factors the Army and Marine Corps consider in determining whether to use live or simulation-based training, including the extent to which they consider performance and cost information, we assessed Army and Marine Corps documentation, such as the 2013 Army Posture Statement; U.S Army Training Concept 2012-2020; Army Regulation 350-38, Policies and Management for Training Aids, Devices, Simulators, and Simulations; the 2012 Army Training Strategy; the Posture of the United States Marine Corps, 2013 Report to Congress; and Marine Corps Concepts and Programs 2013. We reviewed Department of Defense (DOD) and Navy Training guidance. We also reviewed our previous reports on Air Force and Navy virtual training. To determine the services' mixes of live and simulation-based training for institutional and home station training, we reviewed Army and Marine Corps policies and guidance related to developing and conducting training, including the Training and Doctrine Command Regulation 350-70: Army Learning Policy and Systems; U.S. Army Training and Doctrine Command Pamphlet 350-70-1, Training Development in Support of the

Operational Domain; and NAVMC 1553.1: the Marine Corps' Systems Approach to Training User's Guide. We interviewed officials from the services' training commands, the Army Reserve Command, the Army National Guard, Marine Corps Forces Reserve, and subject matter experts for the selected occupations to discuss the mix of training at institutions and home station for active and reserve component personnel, how these mixes are developed, and the factors that are considered. We reviewed programs of instruction to obtain examples of the mixes of live and simulation-based training prescribed during institutional training in the selected occupations. To determine the services' mix of training at home station we reviewed examples of the Army Combined Arms Training Strategies, Army proponent's Home Station Gated Training Strategies, and the Marine Corps' Training and Readiness Manuals. We also interviewed officials from the Army Reserve and Army National Guard, as well as unit commanders and officials from the installations that we visited, i.e., Army's 3rd Brigade, 3rd Infantry Division at Fort Benning, Georgia; 1st Air Cavalry Brigade, 1st Calvary Division, at Fort Hood, Texas; 31st Air Defense Artillery Brigade, 75th Fires Brigade, and 214th Fires Brigade at Fort Sill, Oklahoma; and former Marine Corps battalion and company commanders and officials from the Marine Corps Forces Reserve to discuss how the Army's and Marine Corps' overarching training strategies assist commanders in developing a mix of live and simulation-based training for home station training. In addition, we interviewed Army and Marine Corps training officials to identify and determine the types of information collected on the use of simulators and simulations; how this information was being used; and how the services determine the relationship between simulator usage and performance. We also obtained examples of the types of information being collected by both services, and participated in an online demonstration of the Army's central repository for this information. In addition, we reviewed the Navy's Overarching Fleet Simulator Strategy and management practices on performance measures. To determine how costs are considered and compared when developing live and simulation-based training, we met with officials from Department of the Army and both services' training commands. We reviewed the Army's 3rd edition of its Cost Benefit Analysis Guide to identify potential DOD criteria as to what factors should be included when conducting a cost-benefit analysis. We also reviewed Army and Marine Corps acquisition guidance, which provides instruction on conducting cost-benefit analyses to acquire simulators. In addition, we reviewed federal internal control standards, our past reviews on the Air Force's use of live and virtual training, and federal cost-estimating and budgeting guidance. Further, we interviewed training officials and current and former unit commanders from both services to further clarify how costs are considered when developing the different mixes of live and simulation-based training.

In conducting this work, we contacted officials from the organizations outlined in table 2.

Table 2: Organizations Interviewed During Our Review

Office of the Secretary of Defense for Personnel and Readiness, Arlington, Va.
Deputy Assistant Secretary of Defense (Readiness), Training Readiness and Strategy, Arlington, Va.
U.S. Army
Office of the Assistant Secretary of the Army (Acquisition, Technology and Logistics), Arlington, Va.
Department of the Army, Arlington, Va.
G-3/7, Management Office – Training Simulations, Arlington, Va.
G-8, Force Development Directorate, Arlington, Va.
Army Forces Command, Fort Bragg, N.C.
Army Reserve Command, Fort Bragg, N.C.
Army National Guard, Arlington, Va.
Army Training and Doctrine Command
Army Training and Doctrine Command Capability Managers—Live, and Distributed Learning Program, Joint Base Langley Eustis, Va.
Army Training and Doctrine Command Capability Manager—Virtual, Fort Leavenworth, Kans.
Combined Arms Center—Training, Fort Leavenworth, Kans.
Army Training Support Center, Joint Base Langley Eustis, Va.
Program Executive Office—Simulation, Training, and Instrumentation, Orlando, Fla.
Fort Rucker, Ala.
Directorate of Plans, Training, Mobilization, and Security—Training Division
Aviation Center of Excellence
G-3 Support Operations
110th Aviation Brigade
1st Aviation Brigade
Fort Benning, Ga.
3rd Brigade, 3rd Infantry Division
Maneuver Center of Excellence
G-3, Operations, Plans, and Training Directorate
316th Cavalry Brigade
Fort Sill, Okla.
Directorate of Plans, Training, Mobilization, and Security
31st Air Defense Artillery Brigade

75th Fires Brigade
214th Fires Brigade
Fires Center of Excellence
Directorate of Training and Doctrine
Joint and Combined Integration Directorate
Office of the Field Artillery Commandant
30th Air Defense Artillery Brigade
428th Field Artillery Brigade
434th Field Artillery Brigade
Fort Hood, Tex.
Directorate of Plans, Training, Mobilization, and Security
G-3 Training, 1st Cavalry Division
1st Air Cavalry Brigade, 1st Cavalry Division
2nd Brigade Combat Team, 1st Cavalry Division
U.S. Marine Corps
Headquarters, Arlington, Va.
Deputy Commandant, Plans, Policies, and Operations
Deputy Commandant, Aviation
Training and Education Command, Quantico, Va.
Marine Air and Ground Task Force Training and Education Standards Division
Aviation Branch
Ground Branch
Training and Education Capabilities Division
Range and Training Area Management Branch
Marine Air and Ground Task Force Training Simulations Branch
Training Command
Marine Corps Detachment, Fort Benning, Ga.
Marine Corps Artillery Detachment, Fort Sill, Okla.
Assault Amphibian School, Camp Pendleton, Calif.
Marine Corps Detachment, Fort Leonard Wood, Mo.
Marine Corps' Systems Command
Program Manager—Training Systems, Orlando, Fla.
Marine Corps Forces Reserve, New Orleans, La.

Source: GAO.

We conducted this performance audit from June 2012 to August 2013, in accordance with generally accepted government auditing standards. Those standards require that we plan and perform the audit to obtain sufficient, appropriate evidence to provide a reasonable basis for our findings and conclusions based on our audit objectives. We believe that the evidence obtained provides a reasonable basis for our findings and conclusions based on our audit objectives.

Appendix II: Comments from the Department of Defense

OFFICE OF THE UNDER SECRETARY OF DEFENSE
4000 DEFENSE PENTAGON
WASHINGTON, D.C. 20301-4000

PERSONNEL AND
READINESS

AUG 7 2013

Ms. Sharon Pickup
Director, Defense Capabilities and Management
U.S. Government Accountability Office
441 G Street, NW
Washington, DC 20548

Dear Ms. Pickup,

    This is the Department of Defense response to the Government Accountability Office (GAO) Draft Report, GAO-13-698, "ARMY AND MARINE CORPS TRAINING: Better Performance and Cost Data Needed to Fully Assess Simulation-Based Efforts," dated July 8, 2013 (GAO Code 351738). We partially concur with items 1 and 2. Thank you for the opportunity to comment.

                                 Sincerely,

                                 Laura J. Junor
                                 Deputy Assistant Secretary of Defense
                                 Readiness

ENCLOSURE

**GAO DRAFT REPORT DATED JULY 8, 2013
GAO-13-698 (GAO CODE 351738)**

**"ARMY AND MARINE CORPS TRAINING: BETTER PERFORMANCE AND COST
DATA NEEDED TO FULLY ASSESS SIMULATION-BASED EFFORTS"**

**DEPARTMENT OF DEFENSE COMMENTS
TO THE GOVERNMENT ACCOUNTABILITY OFFICE RECOMMENDATIONS**

RECOMMENDATION 1: To improve decision makers' abilities to make fully informed
decisions concerning whether training requirements can be met with live and/or simulation-based
training and determine optimal mixes of live and simulation-based training, the GAO
recommends that the Secretary of Defense direct that the Secretary of the Army and the
Commandant of the Marine Corps to develop outcome-oriented performance metrics that can be
used to assess the impact of simulation-based training on improving the performance or
proficiency of service members and units.

DOD RESPONSE: Partially concur. The Department of Defense (DoD) agrees an
enhancement in outcome-oriented performance metrics would be helpful in the decision-making
process. However, given the magnitude and scope of training tasks, varying competencies of the
training audience, and ever-changing technology, the problem set contains many independent
variables. The DoD will study the problem set, and as appropriate, develop a construct and
implementation plan to include performance metrics to assess the impact of simulation-based
training on service members and unit proficiency.

RECOMMENDATION 2: To improve decision makers' abilities to make fully informed
decisions concerning whether training requirements can be met with live and/or simulation-based
training and determine optimal mixes of live and simulation-based training, the GAO
recommends that the Secretary of Defense direct that the Secretary of the Army and the
Commandant of the Marine Corps to develop a methodology-to include identifying the costs that
should be included and how these costs should be captured-for comparing the costs associated
with the use of live and simulation-based training.

DOD RESPONSE: Partially concur. The Army and Marine Corps capture all relevant costs
needed for decision making during the Planning, Programming, Budgeting and Execution
(PPBE) process in procuring simulators/simulation devices. Furthermore, the Marine Corps
training is based on the Systems Approach to Training (SAT). SAT includes policy on
developing outcome-oriented performance metrics that are employed in school house lesson
plans and home station training. The combination of PPBE and SAT ensures that costs are
considered in determining the mix of live and simulated based training. The Army and USMC
concur a more comprehensive comparative cost analysis would assist decision making in
determining the optimal mix of live and simulation-based training.

Appendix III: GAO Contact and Staff Acknowledgments

GAO Contact	Sharon Pickup, (202) 512-9619 or pickups@gao.gov.
Staff Acknowledgments	In addition to the contact named above, key contributors to this report were Michael Ferren, Assistant Director; Richard Burkard; Kenya Jones; Jeff Rankin; Michael Silver; Susan Tindall; Erik Wilkins-McKee; and Richard Winsor.

GAO's Mission	The Government Accountability Office, the audit, evaluation, and investigative arm of Congress, exists to support Congress in meeting its constitutional responsibilities and to help improve the performance and accountability of the federal government for the American people. GAO examines the use of public funds; evaluates federal programs and policies; and provides analyses, recommendations, and other assistance to help Congress make informed oversight, policy, and funding decisions. GAO's commitment to good government is reflected in its core values of accountability, integrity, and reliability.
Obtaining Copies of GAO Reports and Testimony	The fastest and easiest way to obtain copies of GAO documents at no cost is through GAO's website (http://www.gao.gov). Each weekday afternoon, GAO posts on its website newly released reports, testimony, and correspondence. To have GAO e-mail you a list of newly posted products, go to http://www.gao.gov and select "E-mail Updates."
Order by Phone	The price of each GAO publication reflects GAO's actual cost of production and distribution and depends on the number of pages in the publication and whether the publication is printed in color or black and white. Pricing and ordering information is posted on GAO's website, http://www.gao.gov/ordering.htm. Place orders by calling (202) 512-6000, toll free (866) 801-7077, or TDD (202) 512-2537. Orders may be paid for using American Express, Discover Card, MasterCard, Visa, check, or money order. Call for additional information.
Connect with GAO	Connect with GAO on Facebook, Flickr, Twitter, and YouTube. Subscribe to our RSS Feeds or E-mail Updates. Listen to our Podcasts. Visit GAO on the web at www.gao.gov.
To Report Fraud, Waste, and Abuse in Federal Programs	Contact: Website: http://www.gao.gov/fraudnet/fraudnet.htm E-mail: fraudnet@gao.gov Automated answering system: (800) 424-5454 or (202) 512-7470
Congressional Relations	Katherine Siggerud, Managing Director, siggerudk@gao.gov, (202) 512-4400, U.S. Government Accountability Office, 441 G Street NW, Room 7125, Washington, DC 20548
Public Affairs	Chuck Young, Managing Director, youngc1@gao.gov, (202) 512-4800 U.S. Government Accountability Office, 441 G Street NW, Room 7149 Washington, DC 20548